MAR 6 2002 Do's

W9-AXZ-058

DISCARDED
From the Nashville Public
Library

Property of
Nashville Public Library
615 Church St., Nashville, Tn. 37219

Hanukkah
Celebrating the Holiday of Lights

Arlene Erlbach

Enslow Publishers, Inc.

40 Industrial Road	PO Box 38
Box 398	Aldershot
Berkeley Heights, NJ 07922	Hants GU12 6BP
USA	UK

http://www.enslow.com

Special thanks to: the Herman Family, Freidel Katz, and Neil Brill.

Copyright © 2002 by Arlene Erlbach.

All rights reserved.

No part of this book may be reproduced by any means
without the written permission of the publisher.

Library of Congress Cataloging-in-Publication Data

Erlbach, Arlene.
    Hanukkah—celebrating the holiday of lights / Arlene Erlbach.
       cm. — (Finding out about holidays)
     ISBN 0-7660-1577-7
     Hanukkah—Juvenile literature. [1.Hanukkah. 2. Holidays.]
I. Title. II. Series.
BM695.H3 E77 2001
296.4'35—dc21   2001000816

Printed in the United States of America

10 9 8 7 6 5 4 3 2 1

To Our Readers: We have done our best to make sure all Internet addresses in this book were active and appropriate when we went to press. However, the author and the publisher have no control over and assume no liability for the material available on those Internet sites or on other Web sites they may link to. Any comments or suggestions can be sent by e-mail to comments@enslow.com or to the address on the back cover.

Photo Credits: © Copyright 2000 PhotoDisc, Inc., pp. 2, 12, 27, 33 (both), 34, 36, 42, 43, 45; Corel Corporation, pp. 8, 9, 14, 15, 16, 21, 23, 29, 40, 41; Courtesy of Nina Rosenstein, p. 30; © 2000, Dover Publications, Inc., p. 24, 26; Enslow Publishers, Inc., pp. 7, 22; Hemera Technologies Inc., 1997–2000, pp. 1, 3, 6, 19 (all), 25 (all); Index Stock Imagery, 2001, pp. 4, 10, 11, 13, 18, 20, 31, 32, 35, 37, 44, 46, 47, 48; Library of Congress, p. 28.

Cover Photo: Index Stock Imagery, 2001 (background); © Copyright 2000 PhotoDisc, Inc., (all inset photos).

CONTENTS

Hanukkah is a happy holiday that lasts for eight days and nights. On each night of Hanukkah, Jewish families burn candles in a candleholder called a menorah.

CHAPTER 1

A Very Happy Holiday

During late fall or early winter, Jewish people celebrate the holiday known as Hanukkah. It is a very happy holiday that lasts for eight days and nights. It begins on the eve of the twenty-fifth day of the Hebrew month called Kislev (which is either November or December in our calendar).

Jewish people sometimes attend parties during Hanukkah. They may play games, eat special foods, sing songs, and give gifts. On each night of Hanukkah, families burn candles in a candleholder called a menorah. A menorah has places for nine candles. One of the nine candles

THE JEWISH CALENDAR

A traditional Jewish calendar is different from the calendar we use every day. The calendar we use every day is based on the cycles of the sun. Each year has 365 days because it takes 365 days for the earth to move completely around the sun. A traditional Jewish calendar is based on the moon. Each month begins when there is a new moon in the sky, and each month has a Hebrew name.

Sometimes Jews go to parties to celebrate Hanukkah. They may play games, eat special foods, sing songs, and give gifts.

is the *shamash*, which means "helper" in the Hebrew language. It is lit first and is used to light the other eight candles. On the first night, the shamash is used to light one candle. On the second night, the shamash is used to light two candles. On the third night, three candles are lit with the shamash. The lighting of one more candle each night goes on until all of the candles are lit on the last night. Another name for Hanukkah is "Festival of Lights."

Hanukkah comes around the same time of the year that Christians celebrate Christmas. But Hanukkah and Christmas are very different holidays. Hanukkah gives thanks for a battle that the Jewish people won more than two thousand years ago against the ancient Greeks. The Greeks, who ruled

over the Jews at this time, told the Jews that they could not practice their religion. They were not allowed to pray in the Temple, their place of worship.

After winning their fight with the Greeks, the Jewish people took back the Temple. Then, they rededicated it to God. The word Hanukkah means "dedication."

Hanukkah is a way to remember a battle that the Jewish people won over two thousand years ago against the ancient Greeks.

The Jewish people follow a religion called Judaism. It is one of the oldest religions in the world.

CHAPTER 2

Who Are the Jewish People?

THE JEWISH PEOPLE

★

These men (below) are praying at the Western Wall in Jerusalem, Israel. Israel is a country in the Middle East that many Jewish people call home.

To understand Hanukkah, we need to know something about the Jewish people. They follow a religion called Judaism. It is one of the oldest religions in the world. Judaism is more than five thousand years old according to the Jewish calendar.

Judaism is the first religion to teach that there is only one God. A wise man named Abraham is considered the father of the Jewish people. Moses is another well-known Jewish person. According to the Bible, God wrote and then gave Moses the Ten Commandments. They are a list of rules for

The Hebrew writing below shows the Ten Commandments. They are a list of rules for living and for worshipping.

living and for worshipping. One of the commandments tells people to honor their father and mother.

Like all religions, Judaism follows certain customs. Jewish people call the places where they pray temples or synagogues. They call

Some Jewish people live in a country called Israel. This is the skyline of its capital city of Jerusalem.

their religious leaders rabbis. Jewish people use only the Tanakh—the Hebrew Bible. The Old Testament is based on the Hebrew Bible.

Some Jewish people follow certain rules about what they can and cannot eat. These people do not eat pork or shellfish. They do not eat dairy products when they eat meat or poultry. They eat only food that is kosher. This means that the food has been prepared in a certain way.

Jewish people observe their Sabbath from Friday evening at sundown until Saturday at sundown. Many Jews celebrate the Sabbath in their home with a special meal. They may also go to temple for prayer services. Some Jews do not work, drive cars, use electricity, or spend money during the Sabbath. This time is meant to be a day of prayer, rest, and study of Judaism.

There are over 14 millions Jews in the world.

Family and friends gather on Friday evening after the sun goes down to celebrate the Sabbath.

Many of them live in the United States. But Jews have also had their own country called Israel since 1948. Its capital city is Jerusalem, and its official language is Hebrew. Many Jewish people who live in North America can read and speak Hebrew, too. Jewish children may be taught Hebrew at religious schools.

Hanukkah honors the Jewish people's victory over the ancient Greeks. But other enemies have also tried to destroy the Jewish people. More than three thousand years ago, the Egyptians kept the Jews as slaves. The spring holiday of Passover celebrates the release of the Jews from slavery. During World

This is the flag of Israel.

In ancient Egypt, Jews were kept as slaves.

14

War II (from 1939 to 1945), German Nazis killed over 6 million Jews.

In spite of enemies who have tried to destroy them throughout history, the Jewish people have continued to live and grow. Hanukkah is a happy reminder of that life and growth.

The spring holiday of Passover celebrated the release of the Jews from slavery. This family is at a seder, a Passover dinner.

These colorful Torah covers are used to keep the Torah safe. The Torah contains books that are important to the Jewish people.

CHAPTER 3

How Hanukkah Became a Holiday

Long ago the Jewish people lived in a land that is now called Israel. In those days it was called Palestine, or Judea. During that time long ago, this part of the world was captured and ruled by many different people. The capital city was, and still is, Jerusalem. It is the most holy city in Israel. The Temple was located there. The Temple was the religious center for the Jewish people. They would visit the Temple and pray to their God. In the Temple, there was a special oil lamp that was always kept lit. It was used to light all the other sacred lights in the Temple. The priests were the

FIGHTING FOR FREEDOM

★

King Antiochus, who fought against Judah and the Maccabees, died the year after the first Hanukkah. But the Jews continued to fight battles with the king's followers for about twenty years. Judah Maccabee died in one of those battles. Jonathan, Mattathias's youngest son, took over. But he, too, was killed. Finally, Simon, the oldest son, forced the invaders out. Israel stayed free for over one hundred years.

A temple or synagogue is a special place where Jewish people pray.

men who took care of the Temple. They made sure the Eternal Light never went out. They kept the lamp filled with special oil that they made from olives. It took over a week to make the oil. No other oil could be used.

Around the year 330 B.C. the Greeks took over Palestine. The religious beliefs of the Greek people were different from those of the Jews. The Greeks did not believe in only one God. They believed that many gods controlled the world. They prayed to statues of these gods. The statues were called idols.

Even though the Greeks had different religious beliefs, they let the Jews pray in peace.

Even though the Greeks had different religious beliefs, they let the Jews pray in peace. Some Jewish people liked the Greek way

19

of life better than the Jewish way of life. They began to practice the Greek customs. Other Jewish people followed their own customs.

In 175 B.C. a new king, King Antiochus IV (AN-TEE-OH-KUS), began ruling Palestine. He told the Jews they had to give up their religion. He wanted all Jews to be like the Greeks in every way.

In 175 B.C., the king of the Jewish people would not allow them to have religious services.

The new king would not allow Jewish religious services to be held. He destroyed religious objects in the Temple in Jerusalem. He replaced them with statues of Greek gods. He ordered the Jews to pray to these statues. If the Jews refused, they would be killed. The king sold some of the Jewish people who did not obey into slavery.

King Antiochus made Jewish people pray to the statues of Greek gods.

Some Jews tried to escape the king's rules by moving away. But they could not hide from the king's soldiers. The soldiers found the Jews who were trying to hide and forced them to give up their religion.

In 167 B.C. some of the king's soldiers came to the village of Modin. There, the soldiers built a statue of Zeus, the king of the Greek gods. The soldiers put a pig near the statue.

Then, they forced the men of the town to stand near the statue.

The Jewish leader of Modin was an old man named Mattathias. The king's soldiers ordered Mattathias to kill the pig and eat it. Mattathias stayed true to his religion and refused.

One man offered to do what the soldiers wanted. Mattathias killed the man and the

Mattathias was a brave man who would not kill a pig and eat it when the king's soldiers ordered him to do so.

Greek leader of the soldiers. Then Mattathias, his five sons, and other Jews in the village killed the rest of the soldiers.

Mattathias and his men left their village and hid in the mountains. Sometimes they came down from the mountains to attack the king's men. They also smashed statues of the Greek gods. They asked people to join them. Many Jewish people joined with Mattathias and his men.

Mattathias refused to kill a pig and eat it.

The rebellion lasted for about two years. Mattathias died during the first year. But, before his death, his son Judah took over. Judah and his men kept fighting, even when things looked hopeless. They continued to "hammer away" at their enemy. Judah and his men became known as the Maccabees.

Mattathias gathers troops to fight against the Greek army.

Maccabee means "hammer." This event began what is known as the Maccabean rebellion.

The king's army was larger than the Jewish army. The Maccabees had only a few thousand soldiers. The king's army had many thousands of men and more effective weapons. The king's men had bows and arrows. The Maccabees had only sticks, stones, and farm tools. Judah Maccabee was a great leader. He made his soldiers believe that God would help them win.

This is a map of Israel as it looks today.

The Maccabees won three battles against the king's troops. The king thought he would finally win if he led a fourth battle. He got together more than twenty-five thousand men, but the Maccabees won again. Then the Maccabees marched to Jerusalem to fix the damage that was done to the Temple.

Judah Maccabee and his men go into battle. Judah took over for his father, Mattathias.

Judah Maccabee and his men removed the statues of the Greek gods from the Temple. They cleaned off dirt and blood that was on the walls. Then Judah went to light the special oil lamp that was supposed to stay lit all the time. It is said that Judah found only enough oil for the light to last for one day. It would take longer than that to make more oil. By what appeared to be a miracle, the oil lasted for all eight days. Judah was able to prepare more oil so the lamp would not go out again. This was the first Hanukkah.

Judah Maccabee and his people had started a new holiday for the Jewish people. It would be celebrated every year and would last for eight days and nights. That holiday is called Hanukkah.

Lighting the menorah for Hanukkah every year is a way for Jewish people to remember the miracle of the oil during the first Hanukkah.

Hanukkah is a special time for family and friends to get together and celebrate.

CHAPTER 4

The Hanukkah Menorah

TEMPLE LIGHT

Today all temples and synagogues contain a light that always burns, much like the light in the first Temple in Jerusalem. This light is known as the Eternal Light.

Just about everyone who knows about Hanukkah also thinks about a menorah. They are thinking about a special kind of menorah called a hanukkiah. It is used only for Hanukkah.

A hanukkiah contains nine candleholders. One of the holders is for the shamash candle. This is the candle that is used to light the rest of the candles. The other candles stand for each night of the miracle of the oil. Only the shamash can be used to light these candles.

There is a certain way to light a menorah. On

On each night of Hanukkah, a special prayer is said while the candles are being lit.

the first night of Hanukkah, the candle in the holder farthest to the right is lit. Each night another candle is placed in the menorah and lit until the eighth night, when all of the candles in the menorah are lit. The candles are always added from right to left and lit from left to right. Each night a special prayer is said while lighting the candles.

The candles in the menorah should be allowed to burn for at least half an hour and should not be blown out. Hanukkah candles are special and should be used only in a menorah. They are a reminder for everyone of the miracle of the holiday. Many families put the menorah near a window for everyone to see.

In many families, people take turns lighting the candles. Sometimes, everyone has their own menorah.

This boy is holding a potato latke. It is a special kind of fried potato cake. People like to eat them during Hanukkah.

Hanukkah is a fun time of year. Jewish children look forward to games, parties, and special foods, like these jelly doughnuts.

CHAPTER 5

Parties, Gelt, and Gifts

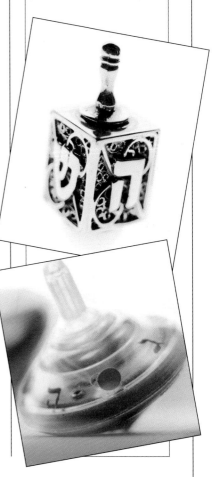

A FUN HOLIDAY

★

Hanukkah is a fun holiday for Jewish children. They can play the dreidel game, go to parties, and eat special foods.

Hanukkah is the highlight of the year for many Jewish children. Today, Jewish children look forward to Hanukkah gifts, games, parties, and special foods. Many children receive *gelt*, money, as a gift. Some children receive gifts on each of the eight nights of Hanukkah. Some families give gifts to each other on only one night. For some families Hanukkah is a time to give gifts to those who are more needy than they are. The gift-giving part of Hanukkah is not an original custom of the holiday. It came from the Christian practice of giving gifts at Christmas.

Many children receive gelt, money, as a gift during Hanukkah. Chocolates wrapped to look like gelt (like these) are also popular.

However, it has become a part of celebrating Hanukkah for many Jewish families. The way families give gifts to each other is different from family to family.

Hanukkah parties can happen on any night of the holiday. Families and friends gather to share the joy of the holiday together. Foods such as *latkes*, or potato pancakes, are served. The latkes are fried in oil as a way of remembering the oil from the Temple in Jerusalem.

Some families eat jelly doughnuts called *sufganiyot*. These, too, are fried in oil.

Some families enjoy eating jelly doughnuts during Hanukkah. The doughnuts are fried in oil. The oil stands for the oil that burned for eight days and nights during the first Hanukkah.

FUN WITH DREIDELS

A *dreidel* is a toy that looks like a top. It has four sides, and a different Hebrew letter is

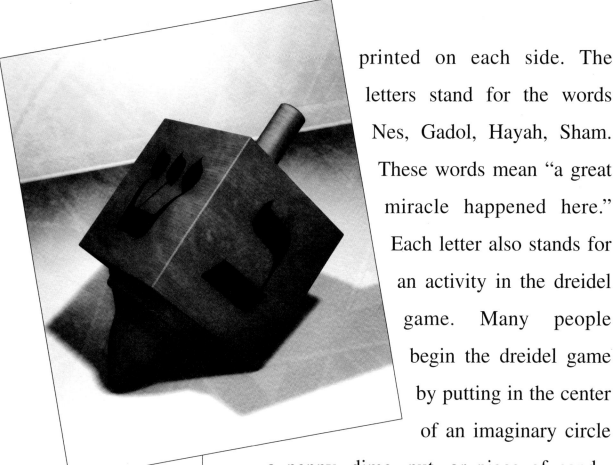

A dreidel is a toy top. It has a different Hebrew letter printed on each of its four sides.

printed on each side. The letters stand for the words Nes, Gadol, Hayah, Sham. These words mean "a great miracle happened here." Each letter also stands for an activity in the dreidel game. Many people begin the dreidel game by putting in the center of an imaginary circle a penny, dime, nut, or piece of candy. Then, each player takes a turn spinning the dreidel. Depending on which letter the dreidel lands, the player takes everything in the center, adds one piece to the center, takes half of what is in the center, or does nothing. Different families have their own special way of playing the dreidel game. Gambling is not allowed in the Jewish religion, but the dreidel game is a fun way to remember the miracle of Hanukkah. No matter how a family celebrates Hanukkah, the lighting of the menorah is at the center of the holiday.

Lighting the candles in a menorah is a special way to remember the miracle of the oil.

Hanukkah Craft and Activity

★

Make a Dreidel

First you will learn how to make your own dreidel. Then you will find out how to play the dreidel game. You will need:

✔ **a ruler**

✔ **a sharp pencil**

✔ **construction paper that is at least five inches long on all sides**

✔ **safety scissors**

✔ **marker pens**

✔ **tape**

= shin

= hey

= gimmel

= nun

*****Safety Note:** Be sure to ask for help from an adult, if needed, to complete this project.

1. Use the ruler and the pencil to measure and draw the outline of a five-inch square on the construction paper.

2. Cut the square out of the construction paper.

3. Fold the points of the square that are opposite each other toward the center of the square.

4. Use the markers to print these words for Hebrew letters on each flap of the dreidel: nun, gimmel, hey, shin.

5. Insert a pencil into the center of your folded dreidel with the point of the pencil facing the ground.

6. Tape the pencil securely to the dreidel.

Hanukkah Craft and Activity

★

How to Play

1. Every player puts in the center a piece of candy, a nut, a raisin, a penny or another small object.

2. Each player takes turns spinning the pencil attached to the dreidel.

3. When the dreidel lands on "nun," that player takes nothing out of the center.

4. When the dreidel lands on "gimmel," that player takes everything from the center.

5. When the dreidel lands on "hey," that player takes half of what is in the center.

6. When the dreidel lands on "shin," that player puts one game piece in the center.

7. Whenever the center is empty, everyone puts in one game piece. The game is played until one player has won all of the pieces.

Timeline

★

330 B.C.—Greeks take control of what is now Israel.

175 B.C.—King Antiochus IV becomes ruler of what is now Israel.

175 B.C. to 168 B.C.—Jewish people are not allowed to practice their religion.

167 B.C.—Mattathias and his sons begin to fight back. The Maccabean rebellion begins.

166 B.C.—Mattathias dies. His son Judah becomes the leader of the Maccabees.

165 B.C.—The Maccabees win their battle with the Greeks. The miracle of the oil at the Temple in Jerusalem takes place.

Timeline

★

165 B.C. to 145 B.C.—New battles are fought with the Greeks.

145 B.C. to about 45 B.C.—Israel is free from enemies.

A.D. 1948—Israel becomes a state.

Words to Know

★

dreidel—A small toy top with Hebrew letters on each side.

Hebrew—The language spoken by the ancient Jews. Some Jews in North America speak Hebrew.

Judaism—The religion of the Jews. It is based on a belief in one God and the teachings of the Old Testament.

kosher—Food that is prepared according to Jewish ceremonial law.

latkes—Potato pancakes that are fried in oil.

menorah—A candleholder used by the Jewish people at Hanukkah.

Words to Know

★

miracle—Something wonderful or amazing that cannot be explained by the laws of nature.

Passover—A Jewish holiday in the spring that celebrates the release of the Jews from slavery.

priests—The men who took care of the Temple in Jerusalem. There are no longer priests in Judaism.

rabbi—A Jewish religious leader who teaches the laws and customs of Judaism.

Sabbath—The day of the week that is used for worship. Saturday is the Sabbath for the Jews.

Words to Know

★

shamash—The candle in the Hanukkah menorah that is used to light all of the other candles.

sufganiyot—Jelly-filled doughnuts.

Tanakh—The Jewish Bible. It was used to create the first part of the Christian Bible called the Old Testament.

World War II—A war fought between 1939 and 1945 mainly in Europe, northern Africa, Asia, and the Atlantic and Pacific oceans. Great Britain, France, the Soviet Union, the United States, China, and their allies fought against Germany, Italy, Japan, and their allies.

Reading About

Bastyra, Judy. *Hanukkah Fun: Great Things to Make and Do*. New York: Larousse Kingfisher Chambers, Inc., 1996.

Clark, Anne, David W. Rose, and Gill Rose. *Hanukkah*. Orlando, Fla.: Raintree Steck-Vaughn Publishers, 1998.

Cohn, Janice. *The Christmas Menorahs: How a Town Fought Hate*. New York: Albert Whitman & Company, 1995.

Corwin, Judith H. *Hanukkah Crafts*. Danbury, Conn.: Franklin Watts, Inc., 1996.

Rau, Dana Meachen. *Chanukah*. Milford, Conn.: Children's Press, 2000.

Simon, Norma. *The Story of Hanukkah*. New York: HarperCollins Publishers, Inc., 1997.

Internet Addresses

★

BILLY BEAR'S HANUKKAH
<http://www.billybear4kids.com/holidays/
   hanukkah/hanukkah.htm>

**THE HOLIDAY SPOT: HANUKKAH
CELEBRATIONS**
<http://www.theholidayspot.com/hanukkah/>

CHANUKAH TIME AT KID'S DOMAIN
<http://www.kidsdomain.com/holiday/
   chanukah/>

Index

★

Index